THE NATIONAL TRUST

By Alison Honey
Illustrated by Peter Stevenson

The Background

This book focuses on life in Britain during the Second World War (1939-45) and the changes that occurred in everyday life for those who were not away, serving with the forces overseas.

'The greatest change the war has made is evacuation. I think it's a horrible idea. The black-out is not at all bad; I think it's rather fun going in the dark. I think we're fighting for a good purpose because if Hitler got all Europe, as he would like to, no one would be happy.'

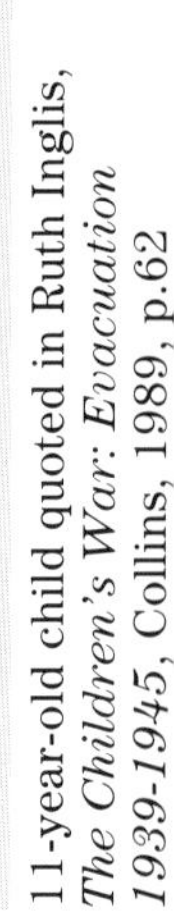

At home...

One important change was the difference the war made to those who lived and worked on large country estates – and to the great houses that suddenly had soldiers or lots of children from big cities evacuated to live in them.

Before the outbreak of the Second World War much of Britain's land was in private ownership, with large agricultural estates in the hands of rich people, living in country houses staffed by lots of servants. They employed many people to work on the land.

But everything was about to change. The estates lost workers as labourers were called up to fight, and houses were left with a skeleton staff as people left to do their bit for the war effort. The Land Army – young female agricultural workers – started to arrive, and many country houses were taken over to be used as hospitals, schools, or billets for troops.

The 'Call up': saying farewell

The war signalled a change in the social order of the country, with people expecting a more equal society. Workers were reluctant to go 'into service' and the old order, with its 'ruling class', could no longer function in the same way. The hardships at home that war created were part of an era of change throughout Britain.

Blickling Hall in Norfolk became an RAF officers' mess

...and away

1939
Britain started conscription (calling up men for National Service).
1 September Hitler, Nazi leader of Germany, invaded Poland.
3 September France and Britain (the Allies) declared war on Germany. British troops landed in France. Refugees from Germany and Austria arrived in Britain. Many were Jews, escaping persecution by the Nazis.

1940
Germany invaded Norway and Denmark and then moved into Holland, Belgium, France and Luxembourg. Winston Churchill took over as Prime Minister in Britain, leading the coalition (all party) government.
British troops were forced to retreat across the Channel from Dunkirk.
Hitler concentrated on destroying Britain's air bases, ready to invade.
8 August The Battle of Britain began. Using radar, Britain could anticipate attacks by the *Luftwaffe* (German Air Force), which failed to defeat the RAF.
Hitler began the Blitz, bombing London and other civilian targets. Italy entered the war on the German side (the Axis powers).

A wartime map of Europe ■ The Allies ■ The Axis powers

1941
Hitler stopped bombing raids on Britain and began attacking the Soviet Union.
The USA joined the Allies after the Japanese bombed Pearl Harbor naval base in Hawaii.

1942
US troops arrived in Britain.
The *Luftwaffe* began the Baedeker Raids on Britain's ancient cities.

1943
Heavy Allied bombing on Germany. Italy surrendered to the Allies.

1944
6 June D-Day: Allied troops landed in France and moved into Germany. Hitler launched the V-1 flying bombs, followed by the more dangerous V-2 rockets.

1945
Dresden in Germany was almost totally destroyed by Allied bombs.
30 April Hitler committed suicide.
7 May Germany surrendered to the Allies.
Survivors freed from the Nazi extermination camps.
8 May VE Day (Victory in Europe).
5 July General Election in Britain, won by Labour.
14 August Japan surrendered after atomic bombs dropped on Hiroshima and Nagasaki.
15 August VJ Day (Victory in Japan) ended the war.

The events outlined here formed a backdrop to the Home Front, which you can start to read about over the page...

Preparing for Attack

When war was declared it came as no surprise. The government had been preparing the population for some time on how life would change and what precautions would have to be made to guard against attack and invasion.

The threat of gas

The British government was convinced that as soon as war was declared Hitler would launch terrible air raids on Britain's major cities, including the dropping of gas bombs. Poisonous gas had been used in the trenches in the First World War and the thought of this horrible weapon being used on civilians terrified people. As a result everyone was issued with a gas mask – babies were to wear huge masks like old-fashioned diving helmets. One man even invented a gas-proof pram.

An adult gas mask: children were given red and blue 'Mickey Mouse' masks

'We all had the standard black ones [masks] except my little sister. She had a red one with a red nose on it that flapped up and down. The one my baby brother was issued with was something like a cradle with a window on top. When Mum put him in it he screamed and kicked up such a fuss, so Mum said, "That's it! If we're going to die we'll all die together." She then threw the gas masks away.'

Jean Carberry quoted in Ben Wicks, *No time to Wave Goodbye*, Bloomsbury 1988, p.40

People soon lost interest in carrying their masks in cardboard boxes with them all the time. Gas was never actually used by either side in the war.

In some areas, even the farm animals were painted so that they would not be knocked down by cars

'Carrots help you see in the dark'

The 'blackout' – where all lights were put out or made virtually invisible – was an effective way of hiding built-up areas which were targets for enemy bombers.

Unfortunately the blackout itself was very dangerous for ordinary civilians as they couldn't see to get about. Cars had to be driven with their headlights masked.

- During the war, 4,000 people died in blackout traffic accidents.
- In the first 4 months, one person in five had an accident in connection with the blackout.

Finding the way

This is how one woman described the experience of trying to find her way in the pitch black:

'There was no moon or stars. I might as well have been down a coal mine. I had to walk about one and a half miles to my home and after bumping into trees, lamp-posts and falling off kerbs, I asked a lady if she could tell me exactly where I was. The answer was, "Hold my arm, dear. I'm blind and I do this walk every day." She knew every lamp-post, tree and kerb and she got me to my home in no time at all.'

Ben Wicks, *Waiting for the All Clear*, Bloomsbury, 1990, p.15

No signposts!

Obstacles were put in fields to stop enemy aircraft from landing and signposts were taken away or painted over to confuse any enemy troops who did manage to parachute in. British civilians often ended up hopelessly lost themselves.

This German fighter pilot, gunned down over Epping, in Essex, in 1940, was confused:

'A young British officer and soldier took me by train to London. On that trip I found out that the names of all the stations we passed through were "Bovril". I didn't know that they had removed the names and left the advertisement.'

Ben Wicks, *Waiting for the All Clear*, p.28

'Careless talk costs lives'

People were warned not to speak to strangers in case they were German spies. A successful poster campaign run by the Ministry of Information showed – in a humorous way – that you never knew who might be listening!

A Safer Place

To avoid as many civilian deaths as possible from air raids, the government suggested moving children (and mothers of very young children) out of the danger areas of London and major industrial cities and into the country, which it assumed would not be at so much risk from bombing. This process was known as evacuation. Sometimes whole schools were evacuated and suitable premises had to be found quickly – these were often large country houses.

Erdington Abbey
Birmingham 23
2nd October 1940

Dear Sir

I should like to convey to you my very deep gratitude for the extremely kind way in which you and your wife have received the children who have been evacuated from my school here. To have one's home invaded as yours has been is by no means a pleasant experience; and I think you have accepted the situation in a spirit of real Christian charity...

When an opportunity serves, I shall pay a visit to the teachers and children, when I hope I may have the chance of thanking you in person for your goodness.

Believe me, dear Sir,
Sincerely yours,
Laurence Hull

This letter was written by the headmaster of a school evacuated to Calke Abbey, a large country house in Derbyshire

Lacock lessons

Lacock Abbey, a country house in Wiltshire, was sent a school from North London with about a hundred pupils. The children lived out with families in the village but came to the Abbey for their lessons.

This is how Mary Talbot, the owner of Lacock Abbey, described the children's behaviour:

'During the five years that the children came daily to the Abbey to do their lessons, their behaviour was exemplary. Sometimes they were left alone in their classroom, but no child ever wrote or drew anything upon the cream-coloured walls, though they must have been tempted to do so. Nor did they break a window, nor pick any flowers on their way between the lodge gates and the Abbey. Except for removing the furniture and hanging linen over the bookshelves in the gallery, we changed nothing.'

Mary Talbot, *My Life and Lacock Abbey*, Allen & Unwin, 1956, p.251

Sleeping arrangements for a school evacuated to a large country house

Another world

Evacuees coming from built-up cities found life strange in the country. Many of the children had never known anything except city life. Often people were shocked by the appearance and lack of hygiene of the evacuated children – many of whom were from the slums of inner cities. Some had never even seen a bath before. Evacuation gave the chance for different sections of the population to mix and be given an insight into different lives and living conditions.

One boy evacuated from Manchester to Tatton Park in Cheshire, in October 1939, collected chestnuts in the park:

'I buy these on Piccadilly for 7 a penny. I didn't know they grew on trees.'

Wartime Tatton, National Trust information booklet

Museums move out

Not only people were evacuated. London's art galleries, museums and record offices were emptied and the contents sent to safer places around the country.

The National Gallery had to find a house with a door big enough for its enormous portrait of Charles I. It ended up in Penrhyn Castle in North Wales and a special container was built to transport it there.

When Penrhyn later became the HQ for the Ministry of Aircraft Production (and therefore a bomb target), the paintings were moved to an underground slate quarry.

Trusty safe places

- **A whole nursery school was evacuated to Waddesdon Manor, Buckinghamshire and all the valuable paintings were moved into the basement.**
- **At The Vyne, in Hampshire, floors were covered with lino to protect them from the boys evacuated there.**
- **Fossils and other specimens from the Natural History Museum were kept at Tattershall Castle in Lincolnshire.**

On the Kitchen Front

During the war, and even for several years after peace had been declared in 1945, food was rationed. Rations were introduced to make sure that Britain had enough food to survive the war. As an island, imports by ship were vital. Apart from the fact that these ships were a prime target for German torpedoes, the British government wanted to keep as many ships as possible for military transport.

'One day my mother had queued for hours to buy a piece of liver for dinner. As she was cooking it on a summer's evening with the kitchen door open to the garden, waves of German bombers came over. She later said, "I thought – my liver or my life?" She chose the liver. She sent me and Dad to the neighbours' shelter and followed later with the liver, plus bits of ceiling plaster which had fallen into it when the bombs fell.'

Ben Wicks, *Waiting for the All Clear*, Bloomsbury, 1990, p.93

'Many people with gardens dug up their lawns so that they could grow more food, potatoes and all kinds of vegetables and fruit. We had no imported food like oranges and bananas… As we kept chickens we had no egg ration but as this was only one egg per person, per week, we did better than that when the hens were laying well.'

Margaret Honey, aged 11 at the outbreak of the Second World War

Dig for victory

Everyone was encouraged to be more self-sufficient in producing food and the phrase 'Dig for Victory' became one of the most famous slogans. Civilians dug up back yards and gardens to grow vegetables, and those who had enough space kept chickens or even a pig.

Many of London's parks were ploughed over to use as productive land.

LEFT Even the moat of the Tower of London was turned into a vegetable patch!

RIGHT Potato Pete (see page 9)

3 pints (1.7 litres) of milk
8oz (225g) sugar
2oz (50g) butter
4oz (100g) margarine
3oz (75g) cooking fat
3oz (75g) cheese
4oz (100g) bacon
1 shilling and 2 pence worth of meat (2 pence had to be spent on corned beef)
1 egg
(in addition to 1 packet of dried eggs a month)
2.1oz (60g) sweets
2oz (50g) jam
2oz (50g) tea

These are the average weekly quantities of rationed food for one adult during the war

Weekly rations

Ration books were issued to everyone. Sausages, bread, potatoes and other vegetables were not rationed but could be hard to come by. Children were given half the adult ration and had their own ration books.

Schools which were evacuated had to make sure the children got their fair share of the ration. The matron of Vinehall School, evacuated from the city to Killerton House in Devon, made sure that each boy's jam ration was put on a saucer labelled with his name and locked away after each meal!

Mock marzipan

8 oz (225g) haricot beans
4 tbs sugar
2 tbs ground rice
1 tsp almond essence
1 tbs margarine

Soak the beans for 24 hours, then cook until tender in fresh, unsalted water. Put them on a tin in a warm oven to get dry and floury. Rub them through a sieve.

Beat the sugar into the bean purée, add the ground rice, warmed margarine and, finally, the almond essence.

Beat until smooth. Any flavouring or colouring matter may be added.

Gill Corbishley, *Ration Book Recipes*, English Heritage, 1990, p.23

Try making this mock marzipan and a peace-time one (find a recipe in a cook book) using ground almonds, caster sugar and egg yolk – see how they compare!

Ration book recipes

Although rationing sounds strict, it was a popular move with most people as it made sure that everyone was entitled to equal amounts of basic food. During the war, diets were in fact healthier than they had been in peacetime and the government introduced school meals and distribution of orange juice, vitamins and cod liver oil to make sure children were not undernourished.

To inspire people the Ministry of Food produced leaflets suggesting ways to use the rations, with cartoon characters, 'Dr Carrot' and 'Potato Pete', who gave helpful hints.
The Ministry suggested that 'mashed parsnips with banana essence are indistinguishable from mashed bananas'.

Dr Carrot

Waste not, Want not

One of the main themes of life was making use of everything available and putting it towards victory against Hitler. People were encouraged to save everything – even bones were important as they could be ground down and used as fertilisers. In London and other cities railings and ironwork were removed to be recycled for armaments.

Norman Longmate, *The Home Front*, Chatto & Windus, 1981, p.167

There'll always be a dustbin,
To save for victory,
So treat it right and let it fight
For home and liberty,
We'll win this war together,
How ever hard it be,
If dustbins mean as much to you
As dustbins mean to me.

Song of the Children's Salvage Corps

Turn your raw material into war material

In 1940 there was an appeal for aluminium to provide material for making new planes.

Lady Reading, the chief of an organisation called the Women's Voluntary Service (WVS), encouraged women to give up their pans:

'We can all have the tiny thrill of thinking as we hear the news of an epic battle in the air, perhaps it was my saucepan that made part of the Hurricane.'

Peter Lewis, *A People's War*, Thames Methuen, 1986, p168

A pie with no meat

Lord Woolton was the Minister for Food during the war and a particularly scrimping no-meat recipe was named after him – Lord Woolton's Pie. Most people had been brought up on a diet of meat and vegetables, so a pie made only of vegetables and pulses did not seem very appealing. Obviously any type of waste was really disapproved of.

Those who have the will to win
Cook potatoes in their skin.
Knowing that the sight of peelings
Deeply hurts Lord Woolton's feelings.

A jingle about Lord Woolton's Pie

Gill Corbishley, *Ration Book Recipes*, English Heritage, 1990, p.4

Warning

Do NOT feed your pig:

Tea leaves, coffee grounds

Banana, grapefruit or orange skins

Paper cartons, dead flowers and feathers

Soda, soap, salt, brine

Rhubarb leaves (poisonous)

Glass, metal or crockery

People who had large enough gardens were encouraged to keep a pig to provide much-needed extra food

Here is an example of a wartime tip:

'Collect wood ash – the clean white kind – to put in a jar near the sink. It makes a good scouring powder and helps to remove stains from metal and china.'

Documents from the Era of the Second World War, The Public Record Office and John Murray, 1993

Sharing a bath to save on fuel

Making savings

The Government issued posters and leaflets with suggestions on how to cope with shortages and make the most out of what was available. Apart from the official rationing of food, clothing and petrol many luxuries were in very short supply. Women substituted cooked beetroot juice for lipstick and used soot as mascara.

Keeping clean also was difficult; there was a soap allowance of 3oz (75g) a month and people were encouraged to have one bath a week which was to be less than 5 inches (15cm) deep. King George VI had a line drawn round his bath to ensure he didn't use too much water!

A long-lasting effect

Rationing became part of people's lives and affected them for years. Meat did not come off the ration until June 1954, 9 years after the war ended.

Make do and Mend

From 1941 clothing was rationed – to free the 450,000 people involved in the textile industries for war effort. Each civilian was given a certain number of points (66, reduced in 1942 to 48 points) to last them the year, and clothing could only be bought by deducting points from each person's allowance.

Clothing coupons

People were able to transfer their points and this often happened in the case of a wedding, when friends would club together to give the bride a dress. In general, clothes rationing was not popular and led to problems for people choosing new outfits without enough coupons.

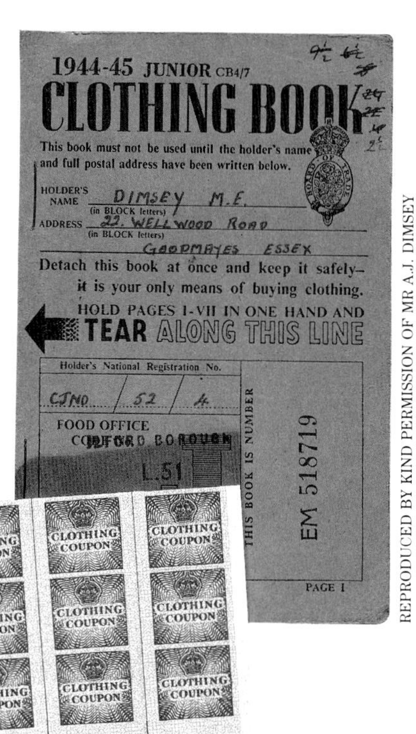

1944-45 JUNIOR CB4/7

CLOTHING BOOK

This book must not be used until the holder's name and full postal address have been written below.

HOLDER'S NAME (in BLOCK letters) DIMSEY M.E.

ADDRESS (in BLOCK letters) 22, WELLWOOD ROAD GOODMAYES ESSEX

Detach this book at once and keep it safely– it is your only means of buying clothing.

HOLD PAGES I-VII IN ONE HAND AND TEAR ALONG THIS LINE

Holder's National Registration No. CJMO / 52 / 4

FOOD OFFICE ILFORD BOROUGH L.51

THIS BOOK IS NUMBER EM 518719

PAGE I

CLOTHING COUPON

Blouse (4 points)
Sweater (5 points)
Slip (4 points)
Suit (18 points)
Shoes with wooden soles (5 points)

Examples of the points needed for items of women's clothing

A little imagination goes a long way

Some materials – such as parachute 'silk' (white nylon) – were not rationed and women became skilled at using all sorts of material to make clothes. Parachute silk was a favourite for making underwear and sometimes wedding dresses. Even household linens were transformed into items of clothing – the popular singer Vera Lynn appeared in a checked dress made out of household dusters.

This is one woman's memory of how she ended up with a new coat after being bombed out of her home:

'They [the Women's Voluntary Service] gave me two great big army blankets and somebody said, "Do you want to have a coat made with that? Mrs Carter will make you one." So I went to Mrs Carter and she made me a beautiful swagger coat and I had it dyed maroon. It lasted for years.'

Peter Lewis, *A People's War*, Thames Methuen, 1986, p.172

Stocking solutions

Nylon stockings were scarce and 6 points from the clothes ration would only buy 4 pairs.

One solution was for women to dye their legs with tea and then paint a thin line down the back of the calf to make it look like a seam!

'We used to put this gravy browning all over our legs and your friend would stand at the back with a black pen or eyebrow pencil and she'd mark a seam down the back. Mind you, if it rained you were in a right mess. The dogs used to come round, sniffing...'

Peter Lewis, *A People's War*, Thames Methuen, 1986, p.168

Tailoring regulations

Jackets: *no double-breasted jackets; not more than three pockets, no slits or buttons on cuffs; not more than three buttons on front; no patch pockets; no half belt, no fancy belts and no metal or leather buttons.*

Waistcoats: *plain, single-breasted only, no collar; not more than two pockets; not more than five buttons; no back straps and no [watch] chain hole.*

Trousers: *maximum width of trouser bottoms 19 inches [48.3cm], plain bottoms, – no permanent turn-ups; not more than three pockets; no side or back straps; no extension waist bands; no pleats; no elastic in waist bands.*

General: *no zip fasteners, and no raised seams.*

The Times, 19 March 1942, quoted in Norman Longmate, *The Home Front*, Chatto & Windus, 1981, p.158

In 1942 rules were issued so that no unnecessary cloth was used

Utility style

As with the food rationing, the clothing coupon system meant that everyone was equally badly off for clothes and people could no longer buy smart new outfits. Winston Churchill set an example by often appearing in public wearing a simple boiler suit – known as the siren suit.

The government introduced a 'Utility' label asking top designers to create a range of clothes out of a limited amount of material, with strict controls over the number of pockets, buttons and pleats. Skirts were straight and cut just below the knee.

The Armed Forces

Some country-house estates played important roles in the war effort. After the Allied retreat from Dunkirk, Churchill ordered the immediate training of 5,000 parachutists. Tatton Park in Cheshire was chosen to be used as part of the No. 1 Parachute Training School set up in June 1940 to train troops and spies in parachute jumping.

Training at Tatton

Tatton's advantage was that the parkland was level with no hills or tall buildings to create an obstacle for parachutists landing. The only problem – described in this song – was trying to avoid farmland, as Lord Egerton had been ordered by the Ministry of Agriculture to plough up over 32 hectares of his land to grow crops for the war effort.

Trainees had to do two jumps from a barrage balloon before they moved on to jumping from a plane. People tended to prefer jumping from a plane, but it was cheaper and quicker to use the balloons.

Oh Mary, this Tatton's a wonderful sight,
With the paratroops jumping by day and by night.
They land on potatoes and barley and corn
And there's gangs of them wishing they'd never been born.

A verse from a Tatton parachutists' song

This is how one person described a jump:

'The misery of the slow ascent to the heavens (800 feet) [244m], the cold, the nauseating [sickening] sway and the deathly silence. The culminating order to jump and the stomach-lifting drop of about 120 feet [36.5m] before the chute opened.'

Compare this to how Evelyn Waugh (later a novelist, but a soldier and secret agent during the war) describes his first jump over Tatton – even though he broke a leg:

'The aeroplane noisy, dark, dirty, crowded; the harness and parachute irksome. From this one stepped into perfect silence and solitude and apparent immobility in bright sunshine above the tree tops... before one had time to do all one had been told, one landed with a great blow.'

Wartime Tatton, National Trust information booklet

NTPL / MARK FIENNES

Tatton Park as it is today

A good idea?

Maurice Newton, 4th Lord Egerton, who owned Tatton Park, often turned his inventive mind on ways to help the war effort. Here is one of his more eccentric ideas, sent to the Home Office, which was not taken up. Its aim was to make the enemy waste anti-aircraft (AA) shells.

Tatton Park, Cheshire, February 1942

...A gramophone or equivalent machine playing a record of the noise of an aeroplane engine. Each machine supported by a suitable balloon. These machines would be carried by bombers; and a few released over enemy towns.

The whole gadget might be designed to blow itself up when the record is finished. This would prevent the enemy from finding out the secret, especially if used over water.

They would be released only at night and only in cloudy weather, to prevent the absence of a real aeroplane being spotted by searchlights. An amplifier would be required.

Letter quoted in *Wartime Tatton*, National Trust information booklet

Over here

American soldiers came to Britain in January 1942 as part of the Allied effort. Their equipment was marked with the initials for Government Issue and so they became known as GIs.

Troop trouble

Armed forces were often billeted at country houses and many properties – although never the target for enemy attack – were damaged beyond repair.

- **Valuable pictures were used for dartboards**
- **Furniture was chopped up and used as firewood**
- **Doorhandles were taken as souvenirs from Kedleston Hall, Derbyshire**
- **Jeeps were driven up wide stone staircases**

'I wanted to see the mausoleum at Blickling [Hall in Norfolk], so Forsyth and I walked across the park to it... We found that the padlock had been forced and the gate opened... The left sarcophagus [tomb] had been hacked with a blunt instrument, and the marble coating prised off the side. Evidently the culprits are the RAF boys who have tried to break open this sarcophagus, believing they would find inside the body of the second countess, who is reputed to have been buried wearing all her jewellery.'

James Lees-Milne, *Ancestral Voices*, Faber & Faber, 1975, p.84

Women at War

When the war started, 6 million women were officially employed – a third of these were in domestic service as nannies, cooks or maids. Very few women had jobs in the 'professions' and even if they did, nearly all women stopped work if they got married. It was considered their duty to stay at home and look after husbands and children; in the Civil Service, leaving the job was compulsory for women who got married. However, from 1939, women were needed to contribute to the war effort.

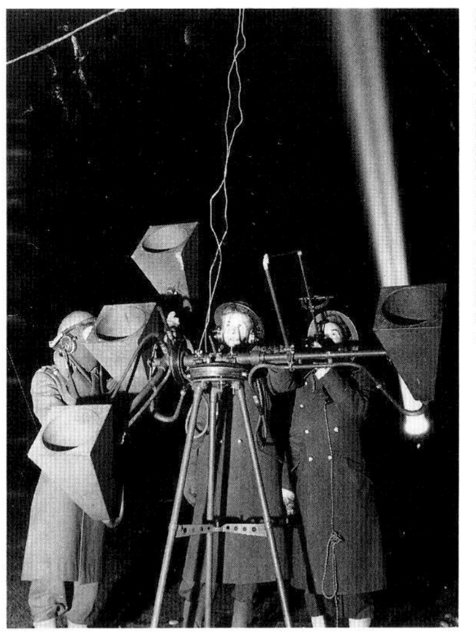

Women helped to guide anti-aircraft fire in the ATS (Auxiliary Territorial Service)

Called up for war work

For many women this was a real liberation and although Britain never allowed women to be on active combat – apart from espionage (spying) – by the end of the war it was realised that there were very few jobs a woman couldn't do.

Britain was the first country to conscript (order) women to do war work; at the end of 1941 all unmarried women aged between 19 and 30 were called up; they could choose between the women's services, civil defence or industry.

Views of life in the Land Army

Peter Lewis, *A People's War*, Thames Methuen, 1986, p.144

'The first week I thought I'd drop dead from tiredness. It was hay-making time. I had two or three blisters on each finger from using a pitch-fork and when we came in at 5.30 the first day, I could hardly stagger up the stairs to bed, I was so tired. And we never seemed to get enough to eat.'

Back to the land

Another key role was working in the Women's Land Army, replacing men who had been called up, and working on the thousands of extra acres of productive land which had been ploughed up since the war started. Recruits had to be aged between 17 and 40, fit and prepared to travel anywhere in the country.

Glamorous recruiting posters ran slogans like 'For a healthy, happy job join the Women's Land Army', showing attractive women wearing crisp, clean work clothes, standing with the fresh country air blowing through their hair.

In the air

Women pilots were allowed only to ferry planes from the factory to airstrips. At first there was a great deal of hostility even to this, but gradually women were accepted and soon they were flying any sort of plane.

Vera Lynn sang in the entertainments service to keep up morale

- ARP wardens (Air Raid Precautions)
- Operating searchlights
- Staffing first-aid posts and shelters
- Ambulance driving
- Firefighting
- Making and operating barrage balloons
- Working in factories and shipyards

Some of the many jobs which were undertaken by women

This is what one woman pilot thought of her war years:

'To be actually allowed to fly brand-new planes before even the RAF got their hands on them was beyond one's wildest dreams. It was five years of absolute bliss.'

Peter Lewis, *A People's War*, Thames Methuen, 1986, p.140

British women have proved themselves in this war. They have stuck to their posts near burning ammunition dumps, delivered messages afoot after their motor-cycles have been blasted from under them. They have pulled aviators from burning planes... There isn't a single record of any British woman in uniformed service quitting her post, or failing in her duty under fire. When you see a girl in uniform with a bit of ribbon on her tunic, remember she didn't get it for knitting more socks than anyone else in Ipswich.

Susan Briggs, *Keep Smiling Through*, Weidenfeld and Nicolson, 1975, p.179

A leaflet given to American troops coming to Britain in 1942

In factories and industry

Women took jobs on the railway, they became welders, mechanics, plumbers, electricians, worked as draughtswomen and in ammunitions. For the first time many women were offered jobs with responsibility.

The WVS

The Women's Voluntary Service (WVS) provided essential welfare for people made homeless during the bombing. They supplied meals and hot drinks and staffed Incident Inquiry Points. Here families, their pets, and any belongings which had survived the attack, could be reunited.

After the war...

When the war ended women were expected to leave their jobs, to be replaced by men returning home. Many women had mixed feelings about this.

The Blitz

In September 1940 Germany launched the heavy bombing air raids which had been feared for so long. The raids, known as the Blitz, followed the Battle of Britain in which Hitler had tried to knock out Britain's airbases and destroy the RAF. Now the aim was to target factories connected with the war effort and to bomb civilians to destroy the morale of the country.

• 250,000 people were made homeless during the first 57 nights of the Blitz.
• Over 20,000 died in the London bombings which continued until May 1941.

The bombing

Of course Britain was not the only country to experience raids. Allied bombing raids on Germany were just as fierce, if not more so, and equally ineffective in achieving their aim. Cologne and Dresden (where 35,000 civilians were killed in one raid) were two German cities which suffered huge losses.

An Anderson shelter

'I remember well the night at the beginning of the London Blitz when the Surrey Commercial Docks in the East End of London were ablaze. Great stocks of timber were set alight by incendiary bombs and we could see to read a newspaper at midnight by the light of the fires twelve miles away.'

Margaret Honey, aged 11 at the outbreak of the Second World War

Sirens and shelters

London was the main target of the bombing and between 7 September and 2 November 1940 it was bombed every night, leaving little time between raids to deal with injuries to people or the damage to property.

ARP wardens and WVS workers worked flat out between raids, rescuing people and finding accommodation for survivors. Warfare was brought right on to the doorstep, something which had not happened since the Civil War in the seventeenth century.

When the sirens went, the official warning that a raid was on its way, people headed for some sort of shelter. Many used the stations and deep tunnels of the London Underground, although this was initially discouraged by the authorities. There were also public shelters and many houses had their own Anderson shelter dug into their gardens.

The Baedeker Raids

These were named after a series of German guidebooks, and aimed at historic British towns that had no military target. They were Hitler's answer to the Allied bombing of historic German cities such as Lübeck and Rostock. Bath in Avon (then Somerset) suffered particularly badly, with many people killed and historic buildings destroyed.

'Miss P. told me in the office that the Bath Assembly Rooms had been gutted by fire in the Bath raid on Sunday night. It has upset me dreadfully that so beautiful a building, hallowed by Jane Austen and Dickens should disappear like this in a single night.'

James Lees-Milne, *Ancestral Voices*, Faber & Faber, 1975, p.52

Kingsmead Street, Bath, following a Baedeker Raid

The terror weapons

A week after the D-Day landings, in June 1944, when thousands of Allied troops arrived in mainland Europe, Hitler launched the first of his 'reprisal' weapons on Britain – the flying bomb, known as the V-1. This was a pilotless plane, loaded with explosive and launched from the French coast with enough fuel to bring it over London. The engine would then cut out and the plane would nose-dive to the ground and explode on impact.

The V-1 attacks lasted for over two months, until the Allies in France managed to capture the launching pads. During this time 5,475 people were killed.

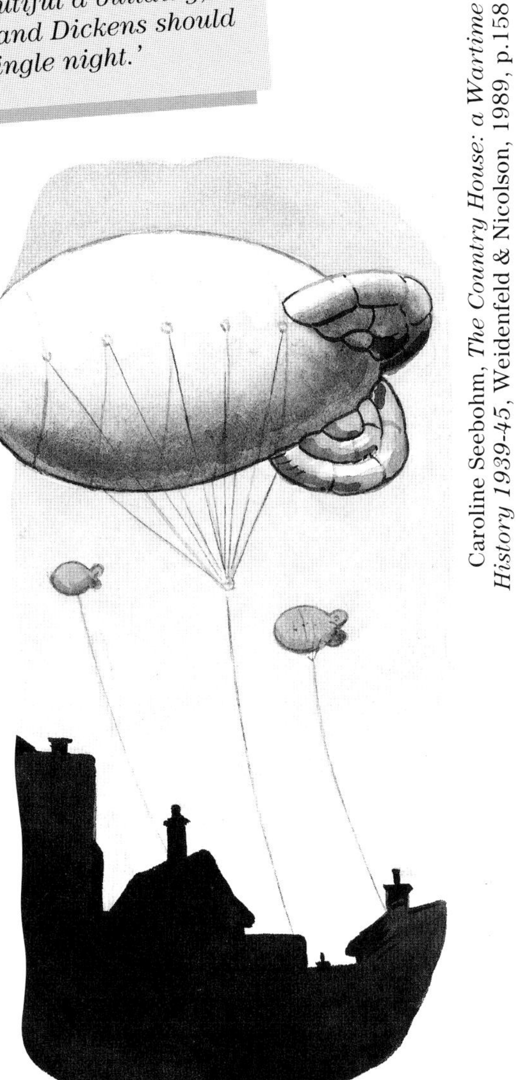

Barrage balloons filled with gas were raised high in the sky, to stop low-flying enemy planes

'This one was headed straight for us and we watched it, paralysed with awe rather than fear. Within a few hundred feet of us the engine cut out... In a breathtaking moment the plane made a sudden curve upwards, flew over the house and detonated in a field a mile or so beyond it. Perhaps Claremont House, like so many beautiful houses in England at that time, had a guardian angel.'

Caroline Seebohm, *The Country House: a Wartime History 1939-45*, Weidenfeld & Nicolson, 1989, p.158

Watching a flying bomb approach over Surrey

Just as people began to get used to the idea of the 'doodlebugs' or 'buzz bombs' as they were known, Hitler launched his next secret weapon, the V-2. This was a supersonic rocket which made no sound until it landed and detonated its ton of explosive.

South Coast Defences

After the Allied retreat at Dunkirk in 1940, the fear of invasion was very real and the south coast of England was strongly fortified. At Studland Beach, in Dorset, tank defences and gun stations were built, and a large old steamship was anchored at the entrance of the harbour, crammed with explosives and ready to be sunk if necessary to stop invading forces. Brownsea Island, in Poole Harbour, also played an important role.

Sea on fire!

An ingenious plan for stopping enemy troops was to set fire to the harbour by pumping oil into the sea and then lighting it. However when this was tried out, the whole village became swamped in thick, black smoke!

Coastline at Studland, Dorset

NTPL / DERRY ROBINSON

A pill box and Home Guard soldier

D-Day rehearsals

Studland Beach was also chosen as the site for rehearsals for the important D-Day landings (and many troops set off from here). Amphibious tanks (which could travel on land and water) were tried out at Studland with mixed success; six of them sank with crew and live ammunition on board. Even today, there are still signs on the beach warning people to beware of live shells.

BOAC flying boats flew civilians out of the country, and also ferried war leaders and VIPs

Brownsea Island decoy

Poole Harbour, in Dorset, was the base for the flying boats of the BOAC (British Overseas Airways Corporation). There was an important factory near Poole which made cordite, a type of smokeless explosive. German bombers were therefore keen to destroy both bases.

The government decided that Brownsea Island could be used as a 'decoy' for the bombers, in a scheme known as Major Strategic Night Decoy, which involved the special effects department from Elstree film studios!

German pathfinder planes would fly ahead of their bombers to locate targets and drop incendiaries (fire bombs). These would show the targets to bombers following behind.

The plan was to fool the bombers into thinking that Brownsea Island was actually Poole by setting off fires on the island which looked like the result of incendiaries, and also creating some realistic fake bomb blasts. The ARP wardens in Poole were very important as they had to put out any genuine incendiary fires before the bombers saw them.

This is a description of how the Elstree special fire effects department constructed their decoy:

'The devices to simulate [fake] the bomb explosions consisted of an enamel bath connected to two enormous tanks, one of which contained diesel fuel and the other was filled with water. The bath was placed over a huge fire made up of about five tons of wood and coal. This fire soon generated an enormous heat when some of the fuel was flooded into the bath. It immediately blazed up and, as soon as this had happened, a sudden gush of water was poured on to it from the tank of water. The water suddenly coming down upon the blazing diesel oil gave the effect of an enormous bomb blast.'

Jack Battrick, *Brownsea Islander*, Poole Historical Trust, 1978, p.133

The decoys were to be set off by detonators but in 1941 they were set off a few times by thunderstorms! However on 24 May 1942, the long-awaited night raid on Poole took place. Fifty-five German bombers flew down the Channel, preceded by pathfinder planes that dropped incendiaries on Poole which were dealt with successfully by the ARP.

The order was given to set off the decoy fires and the enemy bombers were tricked into bombing the island. That night over 200 bombs exploded on Brownsea completely destroying the old village of Maryland and setting acres of forest on fire.

The decoy had succeeded. However the Germans were not fooled the next time – they ignored Brownsea and went on to bomb the cordite factory.

The Home Guard

Many leapt at the chance to do their bit in guarding the home country against possible invasion. Veterans from the First World War turned up to enrol wearing their old uniforms and the oldest recorded Home Guarder was an 80-year-old Scot who had fought in the battle of Khartoum in 1884! As their name suggests, the role of the Home Guard was to keep watch over their specific areas. A key task was night-watching, looking out for any enemy parachutists landing.

'We want large numbers of men who are not at present engaged in military service between the ages of seventeen and sixty-five to come forward and offer their services to make assurance doubly sure... You will not be paid but you will receive uniform and will be armed.'

Anthony Eden, War Minister, 14 May 1940, quoted in Peter Lewis, *A People's War*, Thames Methuen, 1986, p.30

Under-armed

The War Minister had promised that the Home Guard would be armed but in the early days they had to make do with a very strange collection of weapons – often supplied by museums!

Some units were given rifles used more than a hundred years before in the Crimean War. Because of this, and the age of its members, the Home Guard was not taken very seriously by the Germans.

Being captured by the Home Guard did not exactly strike fear into the hearts of the enemy. This is what one German pilot remembers seeing as he baled out from his plane:

'I was swinging down in my parachute in a tricky wind and bleeding from a head wound. I looked down and laughed uproariously at the antics of the British Home Guard down below. They had their eyes on me and were constantly falling in ditches as they ran this way and that.'

Ben Wicks, *Waiting for the All Clear*, Bloomsbury, 1990, p.36

'Churchill has spoken about the Home Guard under arms. We ask – under what arms? Broomsticks? Or the arms of the local pub with pots of beer and darts in their hands?'

A German radio broadcast

Training for the Home Guarders

Sir Edward Hulton, the publisher of *Picture Post*, realised that what was missing was some sort of proper training, so he donated funds to set up a private Home Guard school. Lord Jersey, the owner of Osterley Park in Middlesex, offered his land as a base.

Home Guarders were taught about ambushing, making home-made weapons and other 'guerrilla' tactics. The school was such a success that the Army set up its own training camps in other areas and Home Guarders practised in operations against regular troops. Their advantage lay in the knowledge of their own patch of ground.

Home Guarders were most useful keeping watch over the coastline, factories and aerodromes and staffing anti-aircraft guns. Over one thousand of them died on duty.

NTPL / VERA COLLINGWOOD

Osterley Park, where Home Guard training was held

'Several platoons, in villages where the necessary curves in the main street existed, worked out their tank-traps and demonstrated them in action, with the remainder of the platoon as spectators. Tanks, as a rule, were represented by private cars, Molotov cocktails and sticky bombs by small bags of soot or chalk (which burst on impact with devastating results), anti-tank bombs by thunderflashes or home-made bombs, and flamethrowers by stirrup pumps.'

L.W. Kentish, quoted in Norman Longmate, *The Home Front*, Chatto & Windus, 1981, p.119

A typical Home Guard exercise

Keeping watch

At its peak in 1943 the Home Guard had nearly 2 million members, but in September 1944, when it was clear that Britain was no longer under any threat of invasion, it was disbanded. Although it was sometimes regarded as a 'Dad's Army', its formation did much for the morale of those who were not able to join the regular forces.

Q: *Why did Winston Churchill broadcast his message on the radio?*

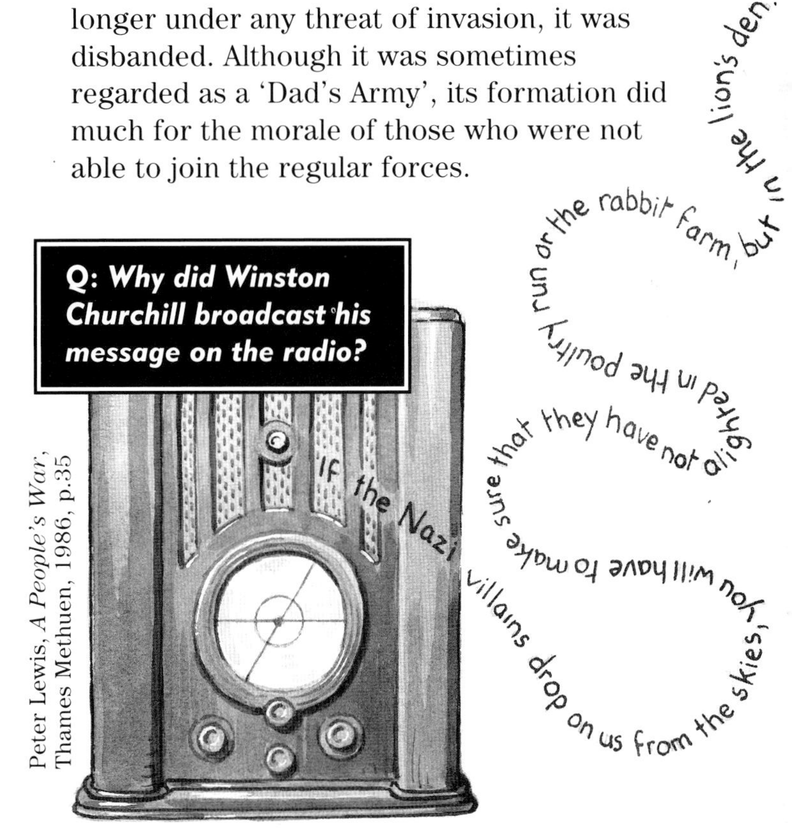

Peter Lewis, *A People's War*, Thames Methuen, 1986, p.35

A *Most people did not have a television*

Family Life

The usual major events in people's lives continued, although people had to be prepared to adapt. If a groom was in the services a wedding could only take place when he was back on leave, often at short notice.

Running to an underground air-raid shelter

For better or worse – wartime weddings

Mrs Jean Williams married her RAF husband while he was back on a 48-hour leave. She wore a blue dress bought with clothing coupons given by friends:

'My husband's mother made a cake with what she could find and we had a tea party at her house. The next day we said Goodbye for a time and he returned to his base to fly in a Lancaster Bomber. Eleven months later he did not return from a bombing trip.'

Leave Permitting, Killerton costume catalogue, 1994

A cardboard cake

Because of the shortage of ingredients, it was forbidden to use sugar as decoration on cakes so icing was not allowed. Couples hired baker's plaster or cardboard models of large tiered traditional wedding cakes to appear in their photographs.

The marriage ceremony could also be quite hair-raising. This is one woman's description of her wedding in London:

> *'Richard and I were married during one of London's heaviest daylight raids. Because of this none of our guests turned up for the ceremony – and, what was more important, neither of the witnesses did. We went out into the deserted street and found two taxi drivers... They acted willingly and charmingly as witnesses... In the evening some friends came in to drink our health but the sirens went very early and most of them had to rush away on duty. We spent the first night of our marriage putting out incendiaries.'*

Frances Faviell, quoted in Norman Longmate, *The Home Front*, Chatto & Windus, 1981, p.80

Christmas

Many children who grew up in the war knew a very different type of Christmas. For one thing, there were no new toys in the shops.

A community Christmas party could be organised by people who used the same air-raid shelter.

'Parents and residents in the street or square concerned clubbed together with cash, or half a pot of jam here, and a bit of margarine there, to provide a tea for the children. ("Bring your own cup.") There were singing and dancing and a film. Some of the wardens made toys from debris wood. We scrounged the paint, and a number of snappy trucks, tanks, and boats were turned out.'

Barbara Nixon quoted in Norman Longmate, *The Home Front*, Chatto & Windus, 1981, p.88

Games and playgrounds

Children made up new games with a wartime theme – collecting shrapnel was popular along with any other war souvenirs. In cities, bombed-out houses became dangerous but exciting playgrounds.

'We lived near Biggin Hill airfield in Kent and used to watch the "dog fights" – British fighter planes attacking German bombers – and collect the used machine gun cartridges from the ground.'

Margaret Honey, aged 11 at the outbreak of the war

Life in a country house

Britain's country houses went through a huge change. Apart from being crowded out with evacuees or billeted with troops, owners found that they had to make do with a handful of people to run their enormous houses, as most of the staff were involved in the war effort.

Knole in Kent is a huge sixteenth-century house with 365 rooms:

'I went to Knole for luncheon. Just Lord Sackville and me. We ate in the large oak-panelled dining-room. He has a butler, a cook and one housemaid who has 250 bedrooms to keep clean.'

James Lees-Milne, *Ancestral Voices*, Faber & Faber, 1975, p.232

Artists and Writers

As in the First World War, it was thought to be a good idea to use artists to record their impressions of the conflict. Several artists were commissioned by the War Artists Advisory Committee to provide a record in pictures, not only of the armed forces, but of how civilians' lives were affected by the war.

War artists

Some of the best-known pictures are the drawings by Henry Moore showing life during the Blitz in the London Underground tunnels. Other artists, such as John Piper, concentrated on portraying bomb damage to buildings.

The Committee was keen to give a positive view of life on the Home Front and show how most civilians were contributing to the war effort. It asked artists to show people at work on the land and also in factories.

Henry Moore described people sheltering during air raids: *'like so many slaves chained in the hold of a ship'*

Ruby Loftus screwing a breech-ring, painted by Dame Laura Knight

Artists showed how women were helping by taking on jobs traditionally held by men. This picture shows a 21-year-old woman who worked in a weapons factory in Newport, South Wales, and was an extremely talented machine operator. The painting was made into a poster and sent to other factories as an example.

War poets

Many poets were greatly influenced by the war but, unlike the artists, there was no committee set up to commission work.

Here is a poem by Wilfrid Gibson dealing with the same subject as the portrait of Ruby Loftus – a woman working in an arms factory – but presenting a different slant, stressing how everyone was brought into the business of war and killing. His poem describes a young mother (maybe even a widow as it mentions her working to support herself and her young son) checking shells before they are sent off for troops to load into guns, to kill.

Shells

All day like an automaton
She fits the shells into the gauge,
Hour after hour, to earn the wage
To keep her and her little son:
All day, hour after hour, she stands
Handling cold death with calloused hands.

She dare not think, she dare not feel
What happens to the shells that she
Handles and checks so carefully,
Or what, within each case of steel
Is packed as, hour by hour she stands
Handling cold death with calloused hands.

Ed. Edward Hudson, *Poetry of the Second World War*, Wayland, 1990, p.15. Reproduced by kind permission of Macmillan General Books and Mrs Dorothy Gibson

The legacy of the war

Many of today's well-known authors were brought up during the war and this provided them with material for books written years after it had ended.

The novelist Nina Bawden wrote her best-selling book for children, *Carrie's War*, about the experiences of a young brother and sister evacuated to a small Welsh village. The writer Evelyn Waugh served as a secret agent during the war and wrote novels such as *Brideshead Revisited* and *Put Out More Flags*, drawing on his experiences.

The writer and illustrator Michael Foreman recorded his memories of life during the war in his book *War Boy*, set in the small village where he grew up. This is his recollection:

'Of course we played "British and Germans" from time to time, but no-one would "be" the Germans, so we couldn't indulge in the hand-to-hand grappling that we enjoyed. We had to be satisfied with long-range sniping at imaginary foes, or a passing old lady. "Dive bombing", with arms outspread, thumbs firing and engine screaming, was a favourite with us and very unpopular with the old ladies. But none of us would ever "be" the Germans.'

Michael Foreman, *War Boy*, Pavilion, 1989, p.48

The Final Months

During the last months of the war the Allies made very heavy bombing raids on Germany, and Allied ground troops fought to push the German army back from the occupied territories. As the Allies advanced, the horrors of Nazism were revealed. Troops discovered the concentration camps where over 4 million Jewish people, gypsies and other groups had been taken by the Nazis and had been starved, experimented on, killed. The surviving prisoners, many forced into hard labour, were very close to death when they were freed.

Searchlights in a V-sign shone over St Paul's Cathedral, London

VE Day

On 30 April 1945 Adolf Hitler committed suicide and a week later all the German command surrendered. 8 May 1945 was declared Victory in Europe (VE) Day and there was much celebrating across Britain. In London, Winston Churchill appeared on the balcony at Buckingham Palace with the Royal Family and addressed the crowd.

Although it was a very happy occasion for many, it was also a day when people whose relatives and friends had died were reminded of their losses.

'This is your victory. It is the victory of the cause of freedom in every land. In all our long history we have never seen a greater day than this. Everyone, man or woman, has done their best.'

Winston Churchill's speech

Arthur Marwick, *The Home Front*, Thames & Hudson, 1976, p.166

'We turned on all the lights, took out the piano, dusted the fairy-lights and strung them on the trees... and gave the kids the best party we possibly could. Two of my friends and I walked down to Chorlton with three empty prams and bought bread, jellies, potted meat, anything we could buy, and filled them until the prams were full to the top. We took tables on to the green... made cakes and scones... we all brought anything out that would burn and had a gloriously, brightly, burning bonfire. That was the end of our war, the housewives' war.'

Mary Smith, quoted in Norman Longmate, *The Home Front*, Chatto & Windus, 1981, p.220

Throughout the war, the ringing of church bells had been forbidden (except as the signal of invasion). At the end of the war in Europe, the bells pealed out again all over the country.

The atomic attacks

In 1940 the Second World War had spread to Asia, when Japan allied with Germany. The war finally ended after American planes dropped atomic bombs on the Japanese cities of Hiroshima and Nagasaki in August 1945.

This was the first time that atomic weapons had ever been used and the result was hideous; 70,000 civilians were killed at Hiroshima and 40,000 at Nagasaki. Facing such horrendous loss of life, and not knowing if the US had more atom bombs to drop, Japan surrendered.

A happy reunion?

The war put a great strain on many families. First, the evacuation, then men away for long periods serving in the army, navy or air force. And the stress of living through six years of bombing; all this meant that many families were split up by the war.

Picking up the pieces was never going to be easy. There were many cases of fathers returning from the forces to children who had grown up while they had been away.

Some fathers returned from the forces to meet a new son or daughter:

'I'll never forget Bill's face as he stood looking down at his small daughter, whom he was seeing for the first time, and at his son who had grown quite different from the baby he had left behind.'

Susan Briggs, *Keep Smiling Through*, Weidenfeld and Nicolson, 1975, p.244

DIEU ET MON DROIT

T

8th June, 1946

I send this personal message to you and all other boys and girls at school. For you have shared in the hardships and dangers of a total war and you have shared no less in the triumph of the Allied Nations.

I know you will always feel proud to belong to a country which was capable of such supreme effort; proud, too, of parents and elder brothers and sisters who by their courage, endurance and enterprise brought victory. May these qualities be yours as you grow up and join in the common effort to establish among the nations of the world unity and peace.

George R.I.

A message to children from King George VI at the time of the 1946 Victory Parade

Back home

Because of the war, women had got used to a new independence. Many were to find it difficult to slot back into the role of a housewife or mother.

A New Dawn

Even before the end of the war, politicians and civil servants were thinking ahead to how to rebuild, and set up the framework for a new Britain.

'There are a large number of people who will tell you that in spite of all the fear, the loss, the suffering, the privation [hardship], the war years were the happiest years of their life. By and large we ate the same rations, we wore the same clothes and we shared a common purpose and there was a sense that this kind of spirit had got to continue after the war.'

Sir Richard Acland, quoted in Peter Lewis, *A People's War*, Thames Methuen, 1986, p.243

Everyone still queued after the war

Looking ahead

The Beveridge Report, published in 1942, proposed a system of insurance where everybody paid the same amount in contributions and in return would get sick pay, unemployment benefit, free health care and a state pension to be looked after in old age.

It was the start of what became known as the 'Welfare State'. Sir William Beveridge, who compiled the report, recognised the importance of improving public health and living conditions, and the dangers of mass unemployment.

Common ownership

Sir Richard Acland, the owner of the enormous Killerton estate in Devon, became a Liberal Member of Parliament in 1935. He was keen on the idea of making society more equal. He believed that 'only under common ownership can we abolish class distinction, unemployment, inequality and strife'. As part of this philosophy, he gave Killerton to the National Trust in 1944.

In 1942, with the writer and broadcaster J.B. Priestley he formed a new political party called 'Common Wealth' which had great success in by-elections during the war. Acland was not alone in wanting a more equal society and there was a general feeling that things could not go back to how they were before war broke out.

New homes were needed

'We are rapidly producing, whether we desire it or not, a classless society – the marks of respect that went to wealth or privilege in the past are going to education and technical skill in the present.'

Captain Quintin Hogg in Peter Lewis, *A People's War*, p.225

All change

During the war there had been a coalition (all party) government. On 5 July 1945 people voted in their first General Election for nine years. Although Winston Churchill, a Conservative, had proved such a great wartime leader, the electorate voted Labour in huge numbers. People appreciated that Churchill had been a great figurehead and inspiration during the war, but were not so sure how his skills were suited for peacetime.

Labour promised Beveridge's Welfare State without delay. Free education, health care and family allowances would now be available – this had not been the case before the war. The new government was also keen to start a programme of nationalisation, under which the major industries would be transferred from private to public ownership and the profits used to finance public services such as the National Health Service (NHS). These ideas appealed to people keen to see a new Britain. Clement Attlee, the new Prime Minister, had a huge task ahead of him because Britain was in financial crisis after the expense of six years at war.

Four million homes had been damaged and half a million destroyed, so there was a serious housing shortage. People were forced to squat in abandoned army camps. Thousands of prefabricated (ready-made) homes were put up. Some of these 'temporary' homes are still used.

Free inoculation in the new National Health Service

Wimpole Hall, Cambridgeshire

In trust for the nation

War had a drastic effect on the lives of all groups of people. The owners of country houses, who had led privileged lives, found their homes taken over during in the war and some property was badly damaged. After the war, such houses faced a very different and uncertain future.

Many owners struck a deal with the National Trust, transferring their houses, their estates (and the income from them) to the Trust, while being allowed to live in part of the property. In this way, many historic places were saved.

Places to Visit

Here are some National Trust places with Second World War connections:

Bath Assembly Rooms, Avon
Bombed in the Baedeker Raids; 1940s costume collection on display and a library with information on wartime fashions

Brownsea Island, Dorset
Used as a decoy for bombers

Calke Abbey, Derbyshire
School children evacuated here from Birmingham

Chartwell, Kent ***(see left)***
Home of Sir Winston Churchill, wartime leader

Cliveden, Buckinghamshire
The house was used as a Canadian military hospital

Lacock Abbey, Wiltshire
School children evacuated here from North London

Lanhydrock, Cornwall
School children evacuated here from London's East End

Osterley Park, Middlesex
Used for training members of the Home Guard

Penrhyn Castle, Gwynedd
National Gallery paintings evacuated here from London; became Ministry of Aircraft Production HQ

Studland Beach, Dorset
Tank defences and gun stations built here; site of D-Day landing rehearsals

Tatton Park, Cheshire
School children evacuated here from Manchester; also a parachute training school

Wimpole Hall
South Avenue was used to guide home bomber crews.

For a full list of National Trust properties, see the *National Trust Handbook*, available from National Trust shops and good book shops.

COVER PICTURES
(clockwise from top left):
Children being evacuated to Lanhydrock in Cornwall;
A ration book (REPRODUCED BY KIND PERMISSION OF MR A.J. DIMSEY);
An air-raid warden rescue;
The Women's Land Army planting potatoes (© IMPERIAL WAR MUSEUM); A child wearing a gas mask; A poster calling for the recycling of kitchen waste (© IMPERIAL WAR MUSEUM);
A Spitfire aircraft.

The National Curriculum

This book looks at Britons at war. It enables readers to learn about the ways in which the lives of men, women and children at all levels of society were affected by the Second World War, before and after 1945.

It takes a look at the ways in which life on country estates – now owned by the Trust – was changed by the war, and how the lives of their owners and staff were altered.

Investigating the Home Front will be useful for children covering Study Unit 3b, *Britain since 1930* (**Key Stage 2**), or Study Unit 4, *the twentieth-century world* (**Key Stage 3**).

First published in 1996 by
National Trust (Enterprises) Ltd,
36 Queen Anne's Gate,
London SW1H 9AS

Registered Charity No. 205846

ISBN 0 7078 0221 0

Designed by Gill Mouqué

Printed on environmentally friendly paper by Waterside Press, England